For Nica

C000058127

Anthony Reynolds

THE PROMOSEXUALS

"To get back my youth I would do anything in the world, except take exercise, get up early, or be respectable."

Oscar Wilde. The Picture of Dorian Gray. (1891)

Portraits of Anthony by Helen Tremaine. London, April 1996. Photo of Anthony & George by Irmin Schmidt. Cologne, May 1996. Most other photographers are sadly unknown.
Copyright © Reynolds, Anthony.
Cover by Kenoshadesign. Layout by Erik Dana Davidkov.
Printed in the United Kingdom.

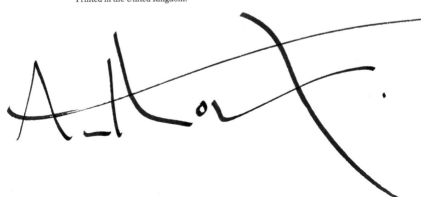

Anthony Reynolds has asserted his right under Section 77 of the Copyright, Designs & Patents Act 1988 to be identified as the author of this work.

Part One:
Europe After The Rain

It's May 1996 and I'm about to embark on my first ever promo tour of Europe. I'm in our record company's (Too Pure) offices at Highbury and I'm being asked prior to the trip who I want to accompany me. Paul Cox, then head chap of our record label is amiably warning me about the upcoming recce. 'It's pretty hard work' he says smiling, rangy, all teeth and lank hair. 'You won't have much time to go off and see galleries and films and things like that. They (the foreign licensees) will work you pretty hard.' Hmm. It seems I don't have much choice in the matter. I'm the singer, so obviously I've got to go. Although for 3 minutes I toy with the idea of granting no interviews - ever - and thus going for a Howard Hughes vibe. This fantasy was quickly scotched. After all, I'm excited! I want to get out there and spread the quixotic word...I can play at being a pop star, stay in hotels, live off room service and theorize with earnest Swedish philosophy students while they interview me for obscure fanzines ... I already have my stock response ready for pretty much any question likely to come up: I'll put my hand to my chin, (I had just the one back then), gaze out of some European window, fix my gaze onto some distantly profound ski resort and quip: 'One wonders...' (I will adapt this in Germany to 'Wim Wenders'). Back in the reality of the North London record company office, the carrot cake munching, lady haired and affable Paul Cox is still talking. Who do I want to join me? Such a trip will be too much for me to bear alone. There's a lot of interest in *Pioneer Soundtracks* and the itinerary will be full. (At this stage I'm not at all surprised that there's so much good feeling about our debut record. It's everything I wanted it to be and more).

So, let's see. Jack is a big group; Seven personnel. I should have a lot of choice, in theory. Audrey, the New Yorker who does the string arrangements and plays violin is nice. We get on OK. She's great at what she does and has a kind of diffuse affability about her; a sort of typical American optimism that I suspect shrouds a deep-seated anxiety. But it's this kind of cheeriness that grates rankly on someone as naturally miserable as I. Richard Adderly, our Rhythm guitarist is another albeit genuinely cheery fellow, seemingly full of the kind of bouncy puppy like joy that comes from what appears to be a healthy middle-class upbringing. (And why not). But he's about 4 years old at this point. While I enjoy the purity of his character in company, helping him to pronounce long words, and mashing up his rusks, he's not exactly a poster boy for the harsh Battaile and Bukowski inspired *Pioneer Soundtracks* ideal. Hmm. Then there's Colin Williams. Bass Player and unacknowledged Frank Zappa Doppelganger. Colin is an enigma to me. Within a riddle. I'm...I'm sort of in love with him. I never feel like I can truly reach him. He's genuinely mysterious to me. A kind of silent guru. What's he thinking behind that goatee and those shades? What's with the smock? Where does he go on weekends and how come I'm never invited? Harrumph. Etc. Nah, Colin is too inscrutable for this trip. Paddy Pulzer, the drummer. Paddy and I just don't mix. It's a chemical/Biological thing. Milk and Poteen. Or maybe it's because at heart I'm a drummer too? And that I don't particularly like his drumming. (It's ok but...more a matter of taste above all...in retrospect I realise I'm just miffed that he's not Steve Jansen.) I Dunno. But whatever... It wouldn't work.

The trip is almost two weeks long. Paddy and I have nowt to say to each other after 10 minutes in the back of a van, let alone over two weeks. Ok. Then howsabout... howsabout...

Matthew? *Jesus*! Forget it. I've never had a relationship like the one I have with co songwriter and guitarist Matthew Scott. He's one of the most brilliant guitarists I've ever heard and one of the most difficult people I've ever met. His social skills are down there with Dustin Hoffman's 'Rain Man' on PCP. We do connect on a deep, mystical musical level, granted. And that's the point. (We're like Jagger and Richards without the revenue). But when we're not playing or writing together, I feel an eerie vacuum rushing in, howling, and making my blood itch and pucker. It's like having a lover and you only bear each other because of the great sex-in this case the sex being the music. After a pint or 30, common ground arises as it would between anyone. I mean, I LIKE him most of the time, even feel a warped and skewed affection for the curmudgeonly bastard. But no way can I share a 2-week trip mano a mano with such damaged, albeit talented goods.

(By the way, whether any of these characters would want to spend two weeks with me...is unrecorded. Their response would most likely be an anagram of the following: "Fop. Not being. That. Cooped. With. Up. I'm"). That leaves George Wright, Keyboard thumper. Big shiny George. George is 6ft 8 inches tall. Very small spaceships orbit his carefully cropped head and his hands span decades. His feet flip flop nonchalantly across varying time zones - heel in the tropic of Cancer - toes in Capricorn. He is also one of the brightest, most articulate and clued-up geezers I've ever met. Much sharper than me. I live in *TonyTown* but George is actually involved in politics and stuff, gets out and moves and grooves in the real world while I make tiny skirmishes upon it and then spend weeks reading and thinking about my excursions.

George is kind of the third genius in Jack (ahem) and like a real true genius; I don't think he's even aware of it. I know Matthew isn't. (There's a vague and sexually potent brooding resentment between them). George's physicality is a big part of his genius as a member of Jack. He looks great on stage, I mean, he looks so wrong for the group he's perfectly right. And even he wouldn't call himself a musician although he has impeccable taste in most things. (Miles Davis was once asked what he looked for in a musician. He replied: '*The way he walks and the way he dresses...*')

But despite being no Chopin, Big G has a true idiot savant talent for noise - of the analogue synth variety. I wanted him aboard originally as a kind of Eno figure but he's something more than that, already...more literary, aggressive and Droog - like and political. Lately he's been wearing a jacket I found in the street, a purple rained on leather thing that only a psychotically depressed Krusty the Clown look-alike could carry off...but on George it looks cool, weird and timeless. It's a look no one else could possibly get away with. I imagine it's hard for him to find clothes to fit, but he saw this in my flat and just claimed it, or rather it claimed him - jumping up onto him like a garishly Puce and elongated stray dog finding its long-lost master. George would be my perfect axis on this promo trip. He can talk up a storm and is constantly surprising and interesting to talk to. The downside is that he can get a bit Argy bargy and unpredictable when he's had a drink or nine. (The line 'There he goes/losing fights in public' from 'Biography of a first son' was written after our first meeting with George. After which he went out with Matthew and ended up surfing down the stairs of some club in a fight with two squaddies while St Etienne (!) played in the background. Big boy agro to the soundtrack of 'Hobart paving'! (Club X I think it was).

But George is cool with me, surely. I'm a sobering influence, right? Of course I am.

So off we go to get our passports - in one day – *the actual day before* and then before Ya know it we're off to Europe.

First stop, Cologne... (Or was it Munich)? Then Holland, France and maybe other places I no longer recall.... The trip will be only a *major* series of fuck ups.

This was the first time I'd flown since I was a kid. I'd flown quite a bit as a child and loved it but that was over a decade ago. I was now worried. For some reason I'd become obsessed with the idea of air pressure. In those days Contact lens saline came in aerosol cans and I was convinced that mine - and for some reason my balls - would explode once in the air. Neither happens. I'm sure I would have made a note if either event had occurred.

Still, I hadn't slept well the night before and was feeling unwashed and slightly dazed when after a surprisingly boring 50-minute flight we arrived in Germany.

However, there was some delay in getting off the plane. A portent of trials to come. George indicated that he wanted us to wait until the rest of the passengers had cleared out. This went against every instinct in my body, an instinct that kicks in on buses, trains and boats – said instinct being to jump up, smash a window and get the fuck outtathere as soon as ready and able. But George kept batting me down, like some fly, fixing his gaze somewhere down the aisle. Eventually I was allowed to leave my seat, the plane now being more or less empty. On cue George bounded ahead with massive elastic strides, goofily approaching an air stewardess. Smiling, he babbled in German (George had, of course at some mysterious point in his young life, lived in Germany). He reminded me of a lethal John Cleese. The air stewardess looked rather bemused at this lanky purple-be leathered Englishman, stooping in the confines of the aisle, his monstrous hands suddenly dwarfing a stub of pen, scribbling something down on a sick-bag. She took the paper gingerly, looked at it distastefully and then nodded kindly at George as if he were a mad giant child.

Eventually the grisly episode was over and we made our way into 'arrivals'. 'What's all that about'? I asked disagreeably, huffing and puffing, pissed off that we were last off the plane for such inane shenanigans.

George was lighting up a fag. His tone - professional and icy: 'I was giving her my number in London, in case she has a stay over'. Jesus. We were not yet officially on German soil and the boy was already on the make...

Outside in the bright clean air, we were picked up by - I don't remember actually - someone from the local Record company (Rough Trade) who seemed as stoic about our visit as we were stoked. The new Teutonic air around us had an exciting foreign tincture. The smell of a million new destinies moving around us... I was a stranger here. George was a strange stranger. It was strangely good to be...strange.

(Boring note: Jack had signed to Too Pure in the UK and Too Pure in turn signed with labels abroad. These labels then license (not merely distribute) Too Pure records. This means they buy the right to press and print copies of, for example, *Pioneer Soundtracks* in their own country. We the group don't see any of this money and it doesn't come off of our debt to the label. So, we may owe the record label £50,000 for what it cost to make *P. Soundtracks* etc. This we pay back by selling copies of the album. But we get only a tiny percentage of the money from those sales to pay back our debt. ("Royalties"). Meanwhile, Too Pure can license the record to 10 foreign labels for £10,000 a time and this has no direct bearing on our debt. This was my understanding of it anyhoo. I stand to be corrected.

And licensing is different to merely *distributing* where a label in Turkey, say, would simply import the UK versions of the record to sell in Turkey).

So, we're in Germany, it's early morning, the car is not, as I recall, long and white. I'm pretty knackered now. My plan is a bath and a nap and then maybe a tour of local bookshops and bars. I've got it all figured out. Because, I mean surely, we're not expected to do interviews *today*, right? Or else we would have come late last night, *right*? This is obvious, logical and civilized. I yawn regally and flop a porcelain wrist about. Hunger pangs begin to bloom beneath my ripped six pack. In all the excitement I'd forgotten I was starving. The driver babbles in German. It's so nice not to know what people are talking about.

I sink back in the soft leather while George lights up a cig' in the front seat.

(It's in my aristocratic nature to always slump in the back of cars.).

'Yeah', I'm thinking. 'A hearty breakfast, Chill out in a steamy bath, siesta, get myself together and hit the town at a little before dusk. Sounds good. I feel lucky. I feel...*good*.' I close my eyes. Everything's gonna' be alright from now on. I'm the boss. I'm running the show. Welcome to *Tonytown*, you scum: Population: *Tony*! On cue I'm awoken by a hard brittle voice from the front of the car: 'Oi! Reynolds!' George turns to me from the front seat all googly eyed and translates: The gist is that we're running late so we're skipping breakfast and getting straight to the job in hand. We don't want to keep the journalists waiting, after all. This then, is German efficiency. "Raus"!!! From this point on, the whole tone, shape and form of every promo trip I'll ever make is patented. And by God, I have no right to protest. Of course, I am grateful to even be here. This is *work,* right? I'm a *lucky motherfucker* that anyone wants to even speak to me about my record, right?

Because, I mean, whom am I kidding? I know, George knows and the guy in the driver seat knows that *Pioneer Soundtracks* is average to middling indie dreck, right? And the small army of Germany's most prominent journalists, now awaiting our presence will know this soon enough too. Suddenly I'm nervous; manicured fingernails in my mouth, flawless white teeth chomping at the quick, I look out the window at the citizens on their way to work. Like they give a schnitzel about our unique blend of melancholic pop rock, right? Fuck. It's a scam. I'm a fake. *A bum*.And everyone knows it. I better get in line boyo! *Fuck breakfast!* Shit. What was I thinking? I shouldn't even be slouching in this backseat.

I sit upright and straighten my tie, tidying my hair. Maybe It'd be better if I offered to drive? I know I can't but I'm willing to learn! Just give me a chance!! *Fuck that* - maybe I should get out without even asking and push the car? Start directing traffic! Christ knows I'm gonna' need a job soon enough! My heart is in my mouth, my blood pressure off the scale...My Dior shirt soaked to my back. I knead the temples of my proud brow with a clammy hand. 'Shit. It's all over before it's begun!' Throughout the entire trip, my lush fantasy sequence of downtime; a breakfast, a bath, hitting anywhere at dusk, never mind Herzog festivals or smoky bars - will evade me. My time is not my own. I will never catch sufficient breath. Again. From this point on I will always be predominately tired, grumpy, frightened and hungry, running with the hunted in pursuit of the mirage of 'promo related record sales'.
(I will embark on promo tours for every Jack album hence and this state of mind/condition will be fought increasingly

with drugs and Tequila. But on this first trip, I am still,
relatively innocent).

We arrive at the hotel; my blood sugar levels - at an all-time
low. The hotel is nice. Stylish. Theatrical. The town is clean.
The mood - efficient. There is a room for interviews with a
reception yonder. I barely catch a glimpse of George and I's
quarters. The journos; eager, earnest, polite, occasionally
challenging, are trooped in.

There is little time to catch breath between the sessions.
While waiting for a phoner to connect - the line is bad - I
cram crackers into my mouth, washing them down with

Coffee, no time even to add cream. Interview wise, I have my spiel down. I don't remember it now, but at the time I was acutely in sync with the philosophy of *Pioneer Soundtracks*. It was a concept album; it embodied a youthful ideal and I lived and breathed it. '*And we both knew something forever/Something now I don't recall',* to quote myself. There was a purity about that time I've never recaptured. So, the interviews were painless in that respect.

The words poured out of me. Automatic talking. What's weird is how natural this unnatural situation felt and so suddenly. This was my life and I was living it. A day of one-sided conversations. Subject: my work - and me -what more could an ego freak like myself want? George was on the periphery of my senses throughout.

Eventually, with dusk creeping up, the last interrogator packed up his Sony and marched off into the evening. Night fell and I was no longer hungry. Just tired and weirded out by having a conversational mirror held up to myself all day. George - a smudge of cigarette smoke and lilac leather - headed out onto the town with the local rep. I skipped dinner and turned in. I hoped to be asleep by the time my buddy got back. George and I shared a room, like GIs. Romantic, huh?

It was cold. It wasn't raining, but I felt like an actor. I lay in the easy gloom and wondered what was going on in Cardiff. I thought of my Girlfriend in London and mused on what the rest of the band were doing at this moment...*The fools.*

Staring through the darkness I was spent and content,
neither horny or not. I wished I smoked. We were going to
another part of Germany tomorrow. I couldn't know it, but
the fuck ups would only happen once we left this country.
London was a hundred years away. I could hear music from a
club down the street. What day was it? I heard shouting in
the evening air. Angry German. Perhaps George had gotten
into some bother with sailors? It was a nice image and I
sloshed it around my brain like mental chewing gum. George
could take 'em and anyway... I was beyond such anxiety.
Knackered. Kaput! There was an old radio on the sideboard,
across from the bed. I turned it on. They were playing *Simple
Minds...*

Part Two:

Mark Eitzel

Soon we were flying to another part of Germany. On a propeller plane! I'm rather nervous. There are only 4 other passengers aboard and the plane is very loud. Being smaller than Yer 'usual commercial flight, it's also very shaky. At one point I asked George to ask the pilot if he could fly a little lower. It seems to me we're getting rather too close to the sun for my taste. George has his noggin stuck in a CP Snow book. I don't exist at such times. So goes the dynamic of our relationship. He ignores me. I start talking to myself, for comfort sake more than anything else. 'Ah well' I muse rather too loudly, 'at least the plane is so empty, if we did go into a dive or whatever, I could make it to that emergency door sharpish. I won't let anyone get in my way. Plus, on a set up like this, I'll wager there must be some provision for parachutes aboard such a jalopy' etc. George doesn't even look up. 'We'd be as good as dead before you had a chance to move' he says calmly. 'Sides which; those emergency doors aren't real in a model as old as this. They're fucking painted on, mate'. Lightly perspiring, I adjust my cravat and get up, moving a few seats further to the rear - out of sight of the damned propeller. I force myself to look at the book I've got: '*Just the One*' - a Biography of Jeffrey Bernard. I'm that edgy I don't read a word. The words swim. I glance along the empty aisles and look sadly again at George, his cropped noggin stuck in his posh book. He seems to be smiling faintly. My thoughts are petty. '*What I would fucking do* Georgie boy, if we started falling out of the sky, is jump on your back like a chimp and then jump off when were 2ft from the ground'.

(A word from George Wright: *"Ahem. What can I add to this stream-of-cons- nonsense? Marvellously entertaining stuff from Anthony, as always. Of course, you didn't have to travel with him – angel faced but petulant, and the worst traveller I've ever met: AR -'The wheels are falling off the plane'!! GW - 'No, they're not, they're retracting, because we're ascending') AR -'Ascending? Like in a horror film?' (etc.)"*

We spent quite some time in Frankfurt. We stayed at some nice Rough Trade chap's lovely house in the countryside. (Gerhard was his name). He plays Hank Williams constantly and it's nice to see the inside of someone's home for a change. Stroke of luck, no pun etc, there's a copy of German 'Playboy' in the drawer beside the bed. A photo spread, black and white, Helmut Newton style. Two women start out boxing and end up fucking. Just like real life! I'm a grateful witness. Ahem. Calms the ol' nerves, what?

After I have, morning comes and I'm taken to town, to the small flat of a younger record Company rep'. He hands me some CDs by a group called *Bismarck Idaho*. They have tiny stickers on them saying; 'Produced by Momus'! 'Oh, I like Momus' I tell him, all innocent like. 'Did his name help sell any'? 'Oh no' groans the young rep, 'Nein. Nein'... The chap looks aghast. He looks gravely out of the window, as if remembering a childhood in the Gulag. 'Nein...Nein'. At some point I - ha ha - tenderly complain at how busy we are. I'm thus told that Germany is our biggest market which is nice to hear but rather rum as well. Because if this is us big then we must be the size of ant dandruff everywhere else.Then again what am I fucking on about? We've only released a few singles, none of which were domestically released outside of the UK. I learned an interesting dynamic: If something is a critical hit in the UK, then it will travel outward, impressing other territories. But this calculus will not work in reverse. Because our first few singles have been ecstatically reviewed in Britain, the foreign press are thus excited too.

I don't know it now, but while triumphant reviews are jolly nice, what counts in terms of sales is radio play or a cinch on a TV advert. Or a movie synch. All three and you're sorted. I am thus haunted forevermore by the 'produced by Momus' sticker, an ill talisman. Still. Although days of talking about myself have become eerily natural suspiciously quickly, I'm still not completely bored by the process. Germany likes us, and, from the tiny segments (A supermarket, a café, a hotel, an airport lounge), I experience, I Like Germany too...

We spent time in Frankfurt and Hamburg. (I think...I'm not sure.) Somewhere we are taken to a Mark Eitzel gig. He is impressively drunk and abusive to the audience. At some point I get a call on the rep's cell phone - still a novelty in 1996. I'm handed a small black brick. The genially languid tones of Paul Cox are on the other line. It seems that Peter Walsh, the sterling chap love boss dude who produced our album, is in Town! What are the odds! We meet at a bar, once the day's exhausting itinerary is completed. (Among which a student neurosurgeon tells me that 'Hope is a liar' made his neck hairs go 'Pssst'. Someone else tells me our songs are pathetic. 'Oh. If you feel so' I reply,' hurt. 'No, I mean like, full of Pathos, JA?') True to form, as we arrive to meet Pete, the waiters are stacking the chairs, on the brink of closing.

In this rather prophetic atmosphere Pete and I embrace while George, in perfect German, orders a first and final round at the bar. Pete is beaming, a sunny blonde presence. He's lost weight. 'I just cut out all fat from my diet' he states plainly. He's in town recording a German group that sounds like 'The Waterboys'. We're all happy at how the Jack album is going. (Although it's not yet released for another month) ...the mood is justified and civilized.

(Pete): *"I enjoyed working with you too. I did not totally enjoy the Black wing Studio vibe and I know that we were slightly restricted by budgets and schedule, but I feel confident that we got the best out of what was available..."*

The experience of recording with someone as gifted, decent and professional as Peter Walsh did in a way spoil us early. And that was almost a year ago now - the perfect summer of 1995. As the waiters lock up the till, Pete and I are planning for the follow-up album. Matthew and I have already written half of what will become 'The Jazz age'. Pete is enthused by my descriptions of the songs, the new direction, the concept etc. 'Budget will always be a problem though' I say. 'We really need orchestras this time round'. 'Fuck it'! He says in all sincerity. 'I'll take whatever they're offering and build a studio on my land. We'll do it there!' It's a plan. Pete lives in a fine Surrey house on some rolling fields. If we record at home, we can take all the time we want. It'll be even more blissful than the *Pioneer* sessions at Blackwing.

Back in whichever German city this is, the staff are chucking us out. We are on a long boulevard. It's dark and rainy. Lights

through mist. Empty wet streets, cars hissing as they pass...
This then, is Europe in the rain. Pete and I embrace. I haven't
seen him since, although we've spoken a few times.

(What ultimately happened is another story. Too Pure
delayed recording and Pete ended up being committed to a
Simple Minds - that band again - project that went on a lot
longer than planned).

Part Three:

And Now Our Troubles Begin

Next stop: Antwerp, Belgium. I know this ain't gonna be good as soon as we arrive at the station. A turnippy looking fellow with a standoffish manner meets us. On a *fucking bicycle*. I'm aghast. George and I, surrounded by our luggage, are, as ever, knackered. I look around incredulously as everyone but us steps merrily into a waiting cab. 'Umm' I dither, (I'm trying to be polite but it's raining and my hair is getting fucked up.) 'There's...a car...right?' 'Oh no' the prick replies slyly. 'It's not far'. I decided to save time and take an instant dislike to this man. The twat tootles ahead on his shitty bike while George and I scurry behind, pulling spitefully at suitcases and shopping bags. (I found a shop in Germany selling some wonderful Cocteau tomes and they're as heavy as buggery). Of course, I now know that there's no such thing as 'not far' in such cases, just like the term 'ten minutes that away' is a hanky of cock-snot. We hurry hot, bothered and wet from mild rain through busy traffic and across bumpy paving and curbs. At one point the suitcase bucks and rears and I fear my wrist will be put out. 'This is a bit off, isn't it'? I shout ahead over the traffic noise, through wet air. The guy actually stops and looks over his shoulder, sneering. 'Momus was here last week. It was good enough for him'. That name again. 'In fact, he sat on the seat and we rode in together'. He's smiling now. My damp brow crinkles, aghast at this idiot logic. 'Yeh, but there's two of us!' says George, getting agitated, sparking up a fag in the rain. 'Err...Didn't they tell you there'd be two of us'? The guy doesn't answer. I fear George will nut him. We trampled on, sweating and parched in the rain. Eventually we collapse into a stuffy office - not even a fucking hotel mind you! ``We're late,' says the fool. 'We will start immediately'.

Despite this, he disappears and George and I sit fuming on a busted couch for 45 minutes being practically ignored by all

in the office. The guy's manner never improves. I don't know
if it's 'cos he hates the record or what. Of course, I don't mind
if he does or not. I'm not that precious. But by Christ, he
should be professional enough to be polite and considerate,
surely. We're his bloody guests and Citizens of the realm to
boot!

There is some consolation. We're much less busy in Antwerp.
They're not as convinced by our brave and audacious debut
as the lovely Germans. Good. I'm glad. I want to go to bed.
En route to the hotel, we make some sort of detour to a grimy
club, where we were hoisted onto a more agreeable host. The
rude guy clocks off. 'Good riddance to bad rubbish' I mutter
when he's safely out of earshot. The new chap sorts us out a
few spliffs for back at the hotel. We're staying at the Ibis on a
big barren square. We check in hastily and at last I luxuriate
in the solitude of having a room of one's own. I check out the
room service menu. Some kind of cocktail for about £13.
Fuck it. I've got a bit of publishing money left. I'll treat
myself. It's yummy. I flick on MTV. George Michael pops up
singing: 'Fastlove' in a shower. I love this song. I unwind my
Cravat, throw it in the corner. I'm so tired. So very weary.
George knocks and enters. We share a spliff. George: 'I'm
meeting the guy later. There's a Combustible Edison gig.
Coming?' Combustible Edison is a modern lounge group of
some description.

Back in Blighty an atrocity known as the *Mike Flowers pops*
are being hailed as the new religion and Lava lamps are
illuminating England's churches...

'Nah, George. I'll have a drink with you downstairs and have an early one'. I'm a boring bastard and I love it. Although not the most boring one here. At the hotel bar the only other punter is a depressed and middle-aged businessman in a linen suit, a Denham Eliot lookalike. Rock and Roll. Between cocktails – just one more before a kip - I dangerously notice the sign behind the bar, the same one plastered all over the hotel. '*Got a problem?* 'it says cheerily. '*If we can't solve it in 15 minutes, the bill is on us!* ' Or words very close to that effect. It's accompanied by a Zen like figure on a cloud. *Interesting.* (And thus, our fate is sealed.)

I bid young George farewell on his gay way and head to my room. My eyes are killing me now - I've had my contact lenses for the best part of the day. I crave my spectacles. Bath and bed. How I long to get my head on that bone-coloured cradle! On cue, the key breaks in the door. (There are actual keys here, not cards). It actually snaps in the lock, locking me out. This cannot be happening. My eyes! No! *Nooooo!*

I take a weary elevator back to the lobby. I explain what I can to the guy behind reception. He's not especially sympathetic. Of course, he offers me another room but there is no way I can get into mine. It's Saturday night and 'No one can come out now, it's too expensive', he mutters glibly. 'But I need my room' I plead suddenly feeling tearful. I point at my bloodshot eyes, adding by explanation: 'My Eyes!'. He shrugs a peasant's shrug of pure indifference. No doing. Too complicated. These things happen. Excuse me, the phone is ringing. Fuck off please. It's obviously someone much more important than you. I take the key to my new room as he gabbles at the phone in something other than the Queen's

English. At least I have a bed. I'll just have to improvise in the optic department I suppose. Someone will be here in the morning. Some locksmith motherfucker. I'm about to let it go but there's a sudden nagging in me noggin. Ye Gods! The sign! Flying downstairs I decide to re-address the guy behind the desk in a courtly manner. I suddenly feel powerful. I turn, in the manner of Nureyev. Perversely benevolent. 'This is some problem, eh?' I ask him, nonchalantly and obviously fucking rhetorically. He looks up, suspicious. 'Yessss, it is a ...problem' he confirms grumpily. (Why does everyone in Antwerp dislike me so)? I continue the hunt. 'And... The problem can't be solved until morning, right?' 'Is correct' he answers 'As I have told you *'Sir'*, it is triple time to pay a locksmith on a Saturday night...it would be as you say, 'more than the worth of my job". He is suddenly very suspicious...scared even and I am impatient. I'm becoming excited, drooling as I close in for the kill.

'I know that'. I counter kindly. 'I understand that'. I'm suddenly a wise old man. Yoda in a suit. I point at the omnipresent sign, the Zen one on the wall. He turns to clock it. '*Yes??*' He seems mortified, as if this has never happened before now. As if I just put the sign up myself. He is gripping paperwork in both hands with such force that the tips of his fingers are white. I show no mercy. He is weak. He has erred. He must pay. 'I lean in; "*So*. There be a *Problem*. You no *fixo* problem. Thus...the bill is on you, correct'!? He looks suddenly very sad although surely, he won't be paying the bill himself, personally...? Ach, I am weakening in my mercy. So, I drive the knife home: 'I can't get into my room. So, you foot the bill, right?' A Pause. Somewhere a child is crying. 'I think so' he half-heartedly confirms, his head drooping, broken by my logic and now on the verge of tears. He is whupped.

Beaten like a gong by the better man: I. It is settled. I am
soon ensconced in my new room. (Smaller than the original I
might add). Within minutes, troops of busboys are pounding
the steps, bearing tray upon tray of cocktails, crisps and club
sandwiches. Fuck it. After my fifth cocktail, consciousness
swimming, I phone down to reception: 'Another four if you
please'. Jesus. That's about £60 in one phone call... I check
the ubiquitous sign. It swims before me: *'The bills' on us'*.
You bet it is, you rude cunts. And so what? I don't make the
rules. And the record company guy treated us abominably.
Fuck 'em. I no longer even acknowledge room service. I have
no cash on me, anyhow. Couldn't tip 'em if I wanted. As rank
after rank of sweating Bellboy lays down the forest of drinks,
I try to concentrate on the other George in my life right now
George Michael, spinning on MTV in heaven above. George
and me. All the young George's. The young dudes. Me, I'm
24. I can make Pianos orgasm. I pee rainbows and JFK is on
the guest list.

I suddenly consider stuffing my cravat into my mouth to
stifle hysterical laughter but this worries me. I may be drunk
but I'm not *nutty*. And what's more. I'm *right*. It says so,
there on the wall. The writings on the fucking wall, bub. *The
wall*. 'Hey teacher, leave those kids alone! 'The sign *says so*.
'A little sign with clogs on...'I am drunk.

And this is how our troubles began.

Part Four:

WHAT THE FUCKITY!?

By the time George comes back from the club I'm a sprawling sodden mess, crooning 'Fastlove' to a glove puppet made from my Cravat. A deposed King among a sea of wrecked glasses and plates, one boot on, one boot off... And yet George is sad. And that makes me sad. A big man like George? With wet eyes! I dontwanna' see a big man cry. Who dared insult thee? *'Imagine the balls on the fucker!'* 'Wazzup G?' I slur matily. 'Have a drink. Try the Pre-War Moet. It's very good. I'll call down, see if the cunts have another bottle...' I'm reaching for the phone already... 'They fucking ignored me at the gig' he laments, lighting a sad looking fag. 'Wouldn't even buy me a round.' I grin raffishly and wag a pissed finger: 'Ha. I'll fucking remedy that, my boy'. I'm onto room service quicker than a 'Fastlove'. We dine and drink merrily. I'm not even sure I explain the broken lock/sign deal. Maybe George just assumes I'm like this in Hotels all the time. Somewhere deep in my conscience, I know I'm bad. But I'm also right, goddammit! *George Wright,* bally Ho! 'Where are the spliffs?' whines George. It's one of the last things I hear. I'm nodding off. 'I left you 3 spliffs'...

The next nasty morning. I awake early. Too early. Eyes like an Ethiopian Vampire. Ouch. I have to reuse my stale contact lenses. I crawl to the shower, kicking off my socks as I do so, sending glasses and bottles tumbling. A hand goes into an ashtray. I wipe it off on half a baguette...

Later, not quite recovered, I scout the square outside the hotel. There is a garage sale of *Titanic* mementoes. Actual lifebuoys and the like. Hardly good for the luck, what? And a bad bloody omen as it turns out. I creep back into the wreckage of my room. I don't-a feel-a -so good. I slumber in the grey Belgium light. It's Sunday. Blech. Just as I'm drifting away, the phone awakes me. I'm tetchy. 'What'! I snap. It's George. He's crying. Again. My attitude softens. 'What's up' I ask in a fatherly tone. 'The bill …" he sobs. "What?' I reply; 'The fucking *cops*'!? George: "No. No. Not yet. The BAR bill. We have a bar bill of almost £400 and they're gonna' make us pay…They won't let us leave…they're shouting at me'. 'What the fuck!'? I toss the phone. God is on my side. And the poster, don't forget the poster. I dress sharp. Suit and tie. (My old room is now fixed. 'Was No problem' says the arse-faced locksmith). Hatefully, I load my Suitcases into the lift. I pull into the lobby, still half – cut but adrenalin doing its job. The remains of Christ knows how many £13 cocktails and how much Nazi Champagne humming through my veins. The lift hits the lobby: 'What fucker said that!' I spout grandly as the doors open, giggling. George looks very sad indeed, huddled and shrunken over by the bastard rep' -the same one who originally met us on the bike. To cut a sordid story short, the chap who was behind the desk last night is long gone. The sign means nothing, obviously. In fact, the sign itself is gone but there's a patch on the wall where it was. What the fuckitty?! So…it seems we have taken the piss. They demand the money. They can't believe George and I don't have it. Our so-called and Porcine manager is on the phone from England. He doesn't even want to listen to my side of the story - i.e., the truth.

The locksmith comes up to us. 'No problem' he smiles like the idiot he is, stubby thumb aloft. *Everyone* is against us. The cunts…

Somehow, eventually we are let out of the hotel. The bastard
on the bike is furious, steam pouring from his hairy cabbage
ears. He just wants to be done with us. Somehow, sometime
the bill will be settled. As long as we get the fuck out of
Antwerp. *Now*! He insists on escorting us on the train to
Amsterdam, leaving his bike chained at the station. 'The
hotel said they will no longer take guests from us. You have
disgraced us. I will see that you and your band never come
to Antwerp again.' (He's right. We don't). As we approach
Amsterdam the mood settles. A sorry episode. But it's over.
'Try and stay out of trouble until you get to Paris' he bitterly
blathers. 'Then-ppht!' -he makes a theatrical gesture with
his stubby hands, washing them of us - 'Do what you will'.
Sounds good to me. Fuck 'em. I'm too hungover to care. I
root in my Gucci bag and come up trumps. At last - my
spectacles! I take out my contact lenses. Relief! The ticket
inspector approaches. He is a foot away. I have opened my
glasses case for all to see. Oh dear. Perched above and
between my specs are the three giant spliffs. The Bike
bastard becomes as red as a hard-on. Incandescent.
Circumnavigating the ticket inspector, he marches me into
the train's crude toilet. 'Flush zem!! He hisses. 'I insist!'
'Couldn't we keep just the one'? I ask gamely. As if! Was this
man ever young? Down the cistern they go. We return to the
coach.

For us, the war in Antwerp is over. Roll on Amsterdam.

Part Five:

IN THE PORT OF

We're met in Amsterdam by yet another grumpy fellow perhaps he's been forewarned of our bad behaviour? If so, like most people he doesn't mention it. Nothing along the lines of *'I know you were arseholes (and arseholed) in Antwerp. None of that on my watch and well get along dandy, Ok lads? Now come on -Enjoy yerselves*!' Rather, he is merely aloof and vaguely disagreeable to us without ever explaining why. But, (sigh), I guess such a reaction should be obvious, right? But look...listen......as far as Antwerp went, for heaven's sake I was only acting according to the sign. I was, theoretically, in the right, right? *I just did what the sign told me to do*. Plus, we're *British*. We're just being 'eccentric'.

(Years later, on a promo trip to Germany for the second Jack album, an escapade that sees Matthew burn down his hotel room after falling asleep with a fag (As in Cigarette) - in his mouth, - and has one rep break down in tears after we innocently ask about getting some coke, (I think the poor lass may have even asked if we preferred diet or regular) - it is explained to me why our antics aren't accepted as simply part of rock and roll's rich loony legacy: 'Maybe if you were Motorhead or something', I'm told... 'But your music suggests sophistication and a certain gentility - we don't expect the same people to be so...debauched and irresponsible)'. I soon realised that another bottom line was; it's ok to wreck hotels, demand toxic substances and puke onto Picassos and beat each other up - if you're selling enough records to pay for the damage. Therein, layeth the rub.)

But, anyway. I'm in Amsterdam again. The last time I was here was in 1992. That was the first time I smoked da 'erb and the last time, (until 2012), that I drank Gin. The trip ended with me being admitted to the free catholic hospital and I'll tell you about it some other time...

Now, back in May 1996, George and I are staying in a nice hotel with a curly stairway and a lovely view of canals and chained up bicycles. We're old pros regarding interviews and photos sessions by now and I take to wearing George's glasses out of sheer boredom. Bit disorientating as I have my contact lenses in - the stairs are a trifle tricky to negotiate but the novelty factor makes it worth it... What's dawned on me at this point is that although I'm now 'officially in music' or whatever, this trip has very little to do with that. Making music I mean. On this trip, all I seem to do is talk and look out of windows while being photographed - just like *Smash Hits* magazine taught me to do as a kid. I miss my guitar and the sense of advancing myself in any real way. This kind of travel seems to compress the mind, not broaden it. The non-stop days of interviews are beginning to feel unhealthily masturbatory...which is really saying something. So, when it's announced that our next stop is a radio station where we are expected to actually do our thing, the prospect is a welcome relief from the relentless verbal jerking off and posing. We hop into a car with Mr. Surly and it strikes me that even this is a new experience - actually driving in a foreign city. Shit. From now, as far as my life is concerned, public transport is a thing of the past. *I'll never open a door for myself again*

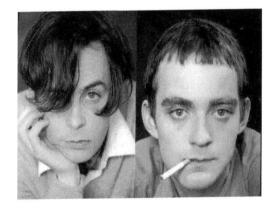

We stop off at a squat where Surly picks up a nylon stringed guitar and then we're pulling into the radio station. It's late afternoon. Just a few hours ago we were somewhere else and soon well somewhere else again but right now we are *here* and I must focus...enter the zone...morph from happy go lucky walker of the world into my higher calling. I've changed into my yellow Adidas tracksuit top, (after Bruce Lee); blue Levi's and vans trainers. I chat a bit with the radio host, a stunningly gorgeous Helena Christiansen look alike. She plays a song from our album and then asks me what it's about. I explain it's the usual - girl meets boy, boy leaves girl for London, misses girl, revisits girl, girl has moved on etc. She gazes at me maternally: 'You know, we girls get upset as well you know'. I focus on her long nylon legs suddenly feeling 13 years old, shuffling my feet and dreaming lusty thoughts...'Yes, I uh, guess so mam.'

After the interview we're shown a barren room. It's surrounded by a much bigger one where another group are fully set up. They peer at us through a window hatefully. So, this is how it feels to be a lobster on display in a restaurant. In our room are a piano and some microphones. The engineer addresses George; 'You're the pianist, right?' G looks sheepish, avoiding the technician's gaze...'Err. Sort of...' George seems dreamy. Preoccupied. The engineer begins his rap: 'It's a lovely Piano. just tuned...nice tone...'etc. etc. George sits on the stool that suddenly shrinks beneath his long frame. He grimaces at the piano, lifts the lid like it was made of excrement and gingerly prods at a key 'Plonk ... plink...' it's obviously a noise making device of some sort... and then he seems to be looking underneath the Piano for something... A Power supply? I think George may be stoned. Tuning my guitar, I call over in my best John Lennon impression: 'You don't have to plug it in George, it's acoustic powered'... We do three songs. 'F.U'. is a four- chord

sequence that doesn't change throughout. That goes Ok.
'Biography of a first son' is less successful, with big G playing
verse chords (To what sounds like another song) as I play the
bridge etc. etc. It feels a lot worse than it sounds. I close my
eyes and think of John Cage eating an apple. I end the
session solo; with a song I've just written: 'This is what you
do'.

(There's a bootleg of this session going about, we don't sound
so bad). Just before we leave, I see a wad of cash change
hands, going from the engineer to Mr. Surly - actually less
surly now that it's apparent they were not complete
monsters. Back in the car George and I ask about the money.
'Oh, it's for the session' we're told. Silence. We're driving
back to the squat to return the guitar. 'Umm...shouldn't we
be having it, then?' George asks innocently. I know it sounds
rude but...well, it's obvious, ain't it? In the driving seat, surly
is obviously improvising; 'Oh, err, no, this is for the hire of
the guitar' 'What! You had to pay your mate to borrow it?' I
ask incredulously. Again, I know it sounds rude but it's not
like we went to a music shop to hire one or whatever..., is it
too much to ask to be paid for our labours? I mean yes, we
would have done it for nowt, but that's not the same as *not*
getting money when we *are* paid is it? And please, brush
aside the argument that such a fee will go against the
immediate cost of our trip, i.e., back to the record company...
It's more likely going in the pocket of Mr. Surly. George and I
are starving troubadours goddammit! Well not *starving*
exactly, we will eat handsomely on this trip...but...Anyway.
Where's my money? I seem to remember us getting half the
fee, the notes counted out there in the street in the grim
European dusk, this seedy act draining the dignity out of our
music making, making it feel like something low and

shameful; George's hand stretching out in anticipation like a rubber gangplank in the moist Amsterdam air... We eat heartily in a restaurant where Mr. not now so surly talks agreeably of nothing but Jansen and Barbieri, who he entertained here just the other month...

Then we wander the streets and with my share of the cash I actually buy a few CDs - Two 'best Of's : Aznavour, Brel, a Paul Quinn album and a Catatonia compilation. Back at the hotel, I am suddenly overcome with exhaustion and a powerful need for solitude. (We're sharing a room again). This leaves poor wee Georgie to venture out alone for the evening. Then again, he's probably better off without me... I'm knackered. I lay against the headboard watching the lights along the river, too tired even to switch on the TV. There's a radio nearby but I decide against it, fearing mid 80's Simple Minds again. I reach out and turn off the light...

The next day we're in Brussels. I remember very little of it, other than me accidently leaving the greatest white shirt in the world in the hotel and leaving too early to buy an amazing Cocteau book clearly on display in a shop window. (I actually scribbled a note with my London number on it and posted it through the shop letterbox. I found the book 6 years later on Charing Cross road). And then we were En route to Paris via a wonderful scenic train trip, chugging slowly through mountains and snow...into the waiting arms of the Gendarmes...

Part Six:

GEORGE GENET

I kept no diaries (other than our songs) and took few photographs during these busy years. There was little time for reflection. I was so embedded in and of my life, I couldn't see it. I vaguely remember the seven-hour Train journey from Brussels to Paris. Alps (?), gorges, valleys, tiny toy towns; George and I goofing around on a lovely old-fashioned train. At one juncture, the dynamic of our relationship had swung so that it is now he who would not stop talking. Instead of replying, I draw a caricature of George on a napkin with a speech bubble saying 'blah blah gibber' etc. I hand it to him. George studies it delightedly. 'Huh!' He exclaims, grinning fruitily. He then screws it up and throws it in my face. It bounces off into the aisles, landing between a professor and a spinster. George thus resumes yapping, the syllables and vowels becoming white noise as my focus shifts to the snowy scene outside the window.

I gaze out at the latest station. Thus begins a fantasy, a fetish that stays with me to this day. From my seat, I watch people embark and disembark from the train. Beyond the station, there's a small village/town. I see shops, streets, alleyways and forecourts, people talking, living...a population of beautiful young mothers, ugly postmen...children on bicycles, regal cats, harassed looking clerks, expensive dogs on long designer leads, old men who shuffle like Nazi war criminals incognito. And I am gripped with a physical urge that makes my legs actually twitch. I want to run from this train into the town and out of this life and into another. I shall walk into a Bistro; buy a frosty German beer and fall into easy conversation with the barman.

As he cleans the glasses and wipes the surfaces his features are friendly, the voice deep and beguiling: 'Oh, Ja, you are English, Ja, ist gut... Zey are looking for an English-speaking man up at Ze University. Bed and board, 1000 deutschmarks a month...Ja, Ja...tell zem Martin sent you...' I follow Mr Borman's advice and soon meet and fall in love with an Agnetha from Abba look- alike. We raise a brood of beautiful, milk fed children. Decade's pass. The years are good to us. Somehow, I eventually become Mayor of the town. *'TonyTown*' as it is now known. Cut to my smoky leather study, the year 2040. I'm sat at my desk, grey, wiry and distinguished looking. A pair of silver half-moon spectacles alight my still handsome face. A knock at the door. English gentlemen. Government officials. In the gloved hands of one of these gents - a Jeremy Irons look - alike, there is a heavy brown paper package. 'Herr Reynolds?' He asks. His tone is serious, that of someone about to deliver either a Nobel peace prize or a bullet to the cranium. 'We have crossed oceans of time to find you...'

Back in the spring of '96, the train crawls out of my fantasy and an unspent life dissolves like a name on a misty Christmas window. Life is slow. Birds fly south. I cross and uncross my legs and knead my temples. We're scheduled to pull into Paris late afternoon. I love Paris. As a boy my family and I went on holiday to Canet Plage. In the South of France, I think? En route we stopped in Paris, near the Eiffel tower and snacked on croissants. It was early morning, misty and out of focus and the atmosphere of the place struck me forcibly. Years later, at 19 I went again with friends. A hollow yet profound trip.

Something about Paris is in tune with my ancient soul, it strums at it like a Gypsy's guitar string...etc

So anyway. I'm most excited because we'll be interviewed by my favourite French magazine... (I only have one) - 'Les Inrockuptibles'. I picked up a fine example of this gorgeous magazine for the first time in 1990 - the legendary Velvet Underground edition. Other copies have filtered through to me since then. All my heroes have appeared in it and now I will. I don't care if we do or don't do one other interview as long as we're doing Les Inrockuptibles.

Back in the carriage, somewhere between Amsterdam and Paris, George has seemingly halted his monologue. I revel in the silence. All is calm, all is still...I lean back allowing myself to relax. George is now looking through his bag, hopefully for headphones. I close my eyes and drift. Maybe the Les Inrockuptibles interview will be a cover feature? I shall have to make some effort before the photo shoot! I want to look my best for all those potential French fans..." My fans... My beautiful fans..." I ease into a doze....

'I can't fucking find it'!!! Far away George is shouting at someone. I ignore him. Behind my eyes, a beautiful rich French girl is handing me the keys to a sumptuous apartment off of the Palais Royale. And this isn't any ol' beautiful French girl. This is Beatrice Dalle, only a little older - just a smidgen, mind - from how she appeared in Betty Blue. She has just opened the enormous doors to a penthouse. 'I want you to 'ave' she says seductively, gesturing to the empty apartment but meaning much more.

'Your vocal on 'Hope is a liar'...how can I say this. It...it...
saved my life. Please accept all...this...as a small token of my
appreciation.' I respond in Jimmy Stewart mode 'Aww,
Gawsh, I, it was nothing, mam, really, I...' The flat is
enormous, chandeliered, mirrored, and elegant. I am finally
getting what's deserved. Finally. I scan the luxurious
décor...saliva glands working overtime... Somewhere far off a
coarse male voice screech: 'I've fucking lost it!' I walk on into
the apartment. Original Cocteau's line the walls. A Picasso
here, a Modigliani there. The place smells of pinewood and
cocaine. I saunter hypnotized into a warm golden bedroom.
There on the four-poster bed is Barbarella! I mean, Jane
Fonda. As she appeared in Barbarella. 'Hi' she says, her
beautiful bright face lit by a powerful inner intelligence. She
strains to address me. But she's actually tied to the bed, face
down and its some effort for her to turn her head, although
not an effort she seems troubled by. In fact, she seems rather
chipper. Glad to see me, no less. 'I've heard all about you', she
smiles. 'Beatrice won't stop playing that darn record.
Mmmm'...She turns to bite the snowy pillow. But not before a
snowy smile. Her smile is a symphony and I feel the stirrings
of great fortune below my YSL belt. On the bedside to her
right is a Balthazar of chilled Champagne, beside it on a silver
mirror, an elegant mound of white powder. Heated oil swims
gently in a crystal tub atop some sort of plinth. In a distant
room Erik Satie himself is playing. Beatrice takes me gently
by the sleeve of my vintage Pierre Cardin jacket. She smiles
sharklike. 'Oh, didn't you know? Barbarella and I are lovers'...
I gulp heavily and glance downward. My Dior shirt is actually
unbuttoning itself of its own accord. My belt pings open.

Somewhere from far off an ugly male voice bellows:
'Awwwwwfucking hell. No! No! Bollocks, I've fucking lost it'...
I snap open my eyes, dissolving the Palais Royale apartment

and leaving Beatrice and Jane to get on with their good and dirty work. George fixes me with those big googly baby blues. He looks ashamed. Holds my gaze. Oh, what fresh hell is this?

'I've fucking gone and lost my fucking passport.'

The train has abruptly pulled into Gare du Nord. The very same train that seemed prettily empty during our journey has now filled this wide station with departing passengers. The walkway is teeming. I focus ahead. My inner voice is turned up to eleven: 'Don't panic. Don't look guilty. Stay cool.' There are a few policemen between us and Paris, stopping passengers at random, flicking through their passports and waving them on. I quickly calculate that they are picking out every 30th passenger. Mostly African fellows. 'What are the odds...' I tell George, feeling wrongly confident. 'They won't pick on us. Not a chance. You stick by me. We'll be fine, boyo'.

As we approach the police, I feel my nerves straining. Inexplicably, my whole body is yearning to distance myself from my doomed comrade. The Reynolds 'Traitor gene' is kicking in, in full force. Part of me wants to turn George in and be done with it. I fight such instinct heroically. We're a few feet away from freedom now, I can smell the coffee and pastries goddammit, and so inevitably, a cop has picked up on my vibes.

He lasers in on George and I, exclaiming wrongness in a hostile sounding foreign tongue. 'I'll distract him,' I hiss to George through flawless Ice white teeth. 'You go on.' I flip open my passport, cracking a rictus grin at the uniformed gentlemen, tilting my head in friendly compliance, shaking all the while. "Ahh, monsieur'...I stutter. 'Uh. 'Ow are you, sir'? Alas, the Cop briefly clocks and then ignores me, heading straight for my 6ft 8-inch buddy, seemingly shinier than ever in his grimy Lilac leather. As George's expressive giant hands weave their protest, accompanied by his broken French, I clock the latest record company rep' who is now approaching, a look of amiable befuddlement on his handsome bald features. Were signed to Virgin records in France - a label I've actually heard of - and here comes their man. What happens next is a long-forgotten flurry of protest, mixed language, huge hands flapping, Black batons being unbuckled from belts and imploring broken syntax. George has disappeared within a crowd of outraged police, his head just visible above the melee. Luckily, the chap from Virgin is a wise and evolved dude. He doesn't freak. As George is dragged off into a blacked-out van and then presumably to the Bastille, the rep seems unruffled and philosophical. I told ya' Haven't I always loved the French? The chap whose name I obviously don't remember shrugs off George's arrest as just another everyday occurrence. Now that's style. As we stroll off, I turn sadly Seeing G's skyscraper frame stooped and forced into a cage at the back of the van, I feel suddenly melancholy. Maybe I should smash a lamp or something and join him? Take off my clothes and wave my second-hand corduroys in protest? 'Spare the boy! Take me instead!'

(George: 'Yes, the curse of my otherwise-so-stylish travelling then was my bloody passport. I'd like to believe it was a subconscious rejection of the whole idea of the Nation State/ no borders, etc, but in reality, it's just a lack of care shouldn't HRH take care of me, with or without that bit of card and paper? So yeah, French cops - they weren't best *pleased. The UK embassy people were lovely – 'it could happen to anyone, old chap'. Incidentally, that purple jacket of Reynolds's served me well through I-D shoots, this trip, random fights at bus stops ('You look like a puff ' - (I stand up - he sits down, 'um, sorry') and so on. I think I lost it about the time I lost my youth...')*

'Ok ' says the virgin Rep coolly. 'Let's go. We're late'. I'm getting used to this now. Forever on the backfoot. I stifle a sigh, as the police van sails off....Who's first?' I ask casually, now the seasoned pro. Already George is a nasty memory. The good die young. So, it goes. My mind wanders...I come to and the rep smiles. 'First we' ave the biggest interview of all......*Les Inrockuptibles!*' 'Sigh'. And so it came to pass that I am photographed for this feature absolutely knackered, unshaven, mop akimbo and in daylight no less. (NEVER be photographed in the daylight). Next to a lemon Citroen. In the photograph I look like a hundred-year-old woman. I am mostly heart broken. The interview goes well though and an hour later, somehow George has joined me unflustered, as if being arrested on arrival to Paris were the most natural thing in the world: 'Just saying hello to the chaps down at the station!' he beams. 'Where's the photo shoot'? In place of a passport, he now sports a stick drawing of a gangly man on a piece of paper with his name scrawled beneath. Albeit signed by the British Embassy. Renaud, the photographer, gets George to pose.Fresh out of jail or not, he's a natural.

Session over, just as in my childhood dreams, we are allowed into the offices of the 'Les Inrockuptibles' and thus help ourselves to scores of back issues. (Although, sadly, the Sylvian issue from 1987 I wanted has inexplicably sold out). (BTW the 'Inrocks' Jack feature is a good piece but we didn't get the cover. The response on publication is muted. Beatrice Dalle never gets in touch. I get little feedback from this coup, other than: James Cook, once of the obscure (and wonderful) band 'Nemo' and now much more popular solo artist than me tells me in 2000 that: *'I was camping in France in 1996 and picked up that issue...I thought, 'The bastard! That's what I*

wanted to say!' Lucy Wilkins, Jack violinist for a few months
once Audrey had left, told me soon after; *'Oh, yah, I read that
on a tour bus in Nantes...I saw the photo and thought: 'He
needs a Stylist'...* In the summer of 2001, I am recording with
Franck Roussel in a steaming hot Parisian Studio. Next to the
couch is that very issue. *' Shit' says Franck, 'You look
younger now than you did then.'*) All else I remember of our
final city on that first press trip is as follows: Eating and
enjoying steak for the last time in my life (until a few years
ago) in a smoky night-time restaurant, near the old prison, a
steak with Pommes Frites and a heavenly blue Cheese
sauce...I've been chasing the dream of that sauce ever since. I
remember ; the tone of the journalists being fresher and
younger than other countries, each one telling me about their
proposed future artistic exploits and how 'Pioneer
Soundtracks' had galvanized them in some way... I recall G
and I being invited to a pretty writer flat (Hurrah! We get to
see someone's home) ...where we watch Rain Tree Crow
videos...

The Virgin rep telling me of his aspirations as a drummer.
Sadly for me they may have come true, as I never saw him
again and my dealings with Virgin went downhill sharply
from then on... I recall at one point, beneath a Tupperware
grey sky, George and I are being escorted past a Parisian shoe
shop. We both stop and gaze lustily at a pair of hemp yes;
they are made from hemp – Van trainers on display. 'Boy, ah
sure wish I could afford them some', we drool... Later, at the
record company office we are treated further to goodie bags
of free records, promos and the like. 'Do you want yours'? G
asks innocently. I take a quick survey. There's not one record
I can imagine ever playing. 'Nah'. On cue, George disappears
with both of our booty. I am mid interview hours later when

he re- appears minus the freebies but wearing a spanking new pair of Hemp trainers.

(George: *'Paris was a dream, Virgin Records France made us feel welcome, gave us all sorts of nonsense promos, some of which I still have, most of which were swapped in a great little shop in the 3rd for crisp Francs, and yeah, I bought some lovely sneakers.'*)

And so, it goes. By the time we are in line to board the flight home I will happily never do another interview again. A Phone call to my Girlfriend, back home in Holloway Road, North London, seems like a missive to some other almost forgotten alternative life. Everything is in order although it seems Melody maker journalist Taylor Parkes has become temporarily homeless and wants to move in as soon as I return... This will at least result in some fine reviews.

And yet. It ain't over 'till it's over, as Lenny said. At some point while waiting to board the final flight, George and I somehow separate. I eventually settle onto a full plane, with just one empty seat glowing conspicuously beside me. Everyone seems eager for us to take off but there's some sort of delay. I flick through the free magazine. I'm royally fond of George, but right now I would quite happily never see him again. Until the next time. Maybe he's copped off with a baggage handler. Whatever. Again, my recurring urge to walk up the aisles and address the pilot directly is kicking in. Sighs, hums and ennui fill the aisles. 'Come on' someone shouts along the way. Other passengers gradually relinquish their manners and start huffing and puffing like the counterfeit human currency they are. 'Oh, for fucks sake.' etc Suddenly A robotic voice fills the air: 'I am sorry for ze delay'... it's the pilot, over the P.A. system. He babbles further while I study the tarmac through the tiny window and fantasize about us crashing into gymnasiums.

And then here he is. Huffing and puffing stylishly along the aisles, to the boos and hisses of the passengers, I present to you - Mr. George Wright. Weighed down with a refuse bag full of Les Inrockuptibles, A wet head, already scuffed hemp trainers, violet leather jacket and there in his other hand, right there, a mangled scrap of paper where a passport should be. He takes his seat next to me, his proud pate gleaming with sweat. I say nothing... Who am I to judge? I nod to him silently in empathy. Continue reading the magazine. Surely that's the last of it... A respectful hush falls within the plane, as if the fellow passengers could read my thoughts.

And then the engines kick in, the plane picking up speed on the Parisian airway. Surely, if there's one last fuck up, its time is now? But no - without warning, we are free of gravity once more. So soon -too soon - we are suddenly unbearably young once again. George and I, both borderline beautiful, fucked and frazzled, flying fearlessly into the future...

Printed in Great Britain
by Amazon